The Amber
Room

CMM Waterstone-Hillier

Listed & Published on www.interestingbooks.store

Check out other exciting titles

Table of Contents

FOREWORD

"The Amber Room" is a fascinating exploration of one of the world's most famous and mysterious artistic works. The Amber Room is a treasure born in the wealthy Sunstone Palace, and its path is one of splendor, battle, loss, and rediscovery. This book will transport you across time and history as I explore the intriguing world of the Amber Room.

The Amber Room's attraction has only increased over time, owing to its centuries-long history. Its elaborate design, which includes six tons of amber, gold leaf, and priceless stones, has awed generations of people. This masterwork, however, has undergone incredible challenges, including its disappearance during World War II. Theories, tales, and arguments abound in the aftermath of its disappearance, adding to the mystery.

But this isn't only a narrative about a lost treasure; it's also about human perseverance and the stubborn spirit. It is about the steadfast will to regain and rebuild what has been destroyed. "The Amber Room" exposes the arduous attempts to put this jigsaw of art and history back together, giving it new life and conserving it for future generations.

In the pages that follow, you'll go on an adventure to discover the Amber Room's mysteries, from its genesis in the opulent halls of the Sunstone Palace to its disappearance amid the turmoil of war. You'll meet the bright brains and expert hands that created this masterpiece, as well as the stories and debates that surround it.

"The Amber Room" is more than simply a narrative about a lost treasure; it's also about human ingenuity, ambition, and the eternal impact of art. Join us on this voyage back in time to witness the Amber Room's creation, rise to renown, disappearance, and triumphant return to the international stage. Allow the amber light to lead you through this enthralling narrative of history, art, and the unwavering spirit of people who wish to preserve the past for future generations.

Sincerely,

CCM Waterston-Hillier

CHAPTER 1

The Sunstone Palace: The Inception of the Amber Room

The Amber Room's narrative starts in the sumptuous setting of the Sunstone Palace, where the foundations of this magnificent masterpiece were constructed. In this chapter, I will go back in time to investigate the Amber Room's beginnings, delving into the architectural and cultural backdrop of its development and highlighting the skilled artisans whose innovative skills brought this unrivaled masterpiece to life.

The Birthplace of Magnificence: Sunstone Palace

The Sunstone Palace was an architectural masterpiece of the 18th century, located in the center of Tsarskoye Selo (now Pushkin), just outside St. Petersburg,

Russia. Its splendor reflected the luxury of Russia's royal court during the reigns of Peter the Great and, subsequently, Empress Elizabeth. The palace was initially built as a vacation house to match Europe's sumptuous palaces.

The Amber Room would be housed inside this magnificent mansion. The magnificent apartments and elaborate hallways of the palace offered the perfect environment for one of history's most spectacular works of art.

The Cultural and Architectural Context

To comprehend the origins of the Amber Room, you must first grasp the cultural and architectural background of the period. The 18th century saw great enthusiasm for the arts, a type of cultural revival in Russia. Empress Elizabeth, who ascended to the throne in 1741, was a patron of the arts and a lover of luxury, and she intended to establish her reign with unrivaled splendor.

The Rococo architectural style of the time was distinguished by lavish decoration, asymmetry, and a concentration on delicate details. The Sunstone Palace was a Rococo architectural marvel, with stucco moldings, carved reliefs, and colorful paintings on its façade. The interiors were equally lavish, with gilded moldings, crystal chandeliers, and beautiful mirrors.

The Amber Room idea evolved against this background of grandeur and aesthetic inventiveness. The Amber Room was more than just a cosmetic project; it represented the Russian imperial court's aim to equal the splendors of European aristocracy

The Master Craftsmen Behind the Dream

The Amber Room requires not just vision but also remarkable technique. Andreas Schlüter and Bartolomeo Rastrelli, both of German origin, designed this exquisite hall. Schlüter, who studied sculpting and architecture, was noted for his creative creations. Rastrelli, on the other hand, was a well-known Russian-Italian architect best known for his contributions to Russian Baroque architecture.

But it was the artisans who meticulously labored on

the exquisite details that actually brought the Amber Room to life. Gottfried Wolfram and Ernst Schacht, German amber artists, created the room's panels out of six tons of amber. Their amber talent was unparalleled, and they converted this valuable substance into exquisite reliefs and mosaics that dazzled anyone who saw them.

The amber panels were further adorned with intricate gilding, mirrors, and diamonds, resulting in an incredible visual display. The walls of the area were coated in amber and gold leaf, giving it an ethereal radiance when lit by candlelight.

The methods used by these great artisans were revolutionary at the time. Amber, a delicate substance, offered a unique difficulty, yet their talent and ingenuity enabled them to produce a masterpiece that defied conception.

Exploring the Intricate Details

To properly understand the Amber Room's grandeur and origin, I will go further into the subtle elements that make this masterpiece so exceptional. The Sunstone Palace, where it all started, was more than simply a canvas for wealth; it was also a monument to the artistry of the period.

The Sunstone Palace's walls were embellished with intricate stucco moldings and carved reliefs. These architectural components were deliberately created to evoke the Rococo style's feeling of movement and fluidity. The Rococo style, with its focus on asymmetry and extravagant adornment, offered the ideal setting for the Amber Room's forthcoming development.

The palace's interior areas were lighted by beautiful crystal chandeliers that reflected light and created a color play. The gleaming chandeliers contributed to the palace's air of wealth and magnificence. This backdrop was critical in emphasizing the radiance of the Amber Room, which would subsequently become a focal point of this magnificent mansion.

The Origins of the Amber Room

The Amber Room, which originated at the Sunstone Palace, was envisioned as a significant effort to surpass Europe's best ornamental art. The plan was to construct a chamber that would be both a fantastic piece of art and a symbol of Russia's burgeoning cultural and creative power.

The critical element for this complex project was amber, a semi-precious gemstone with a warm, golden tint. This was not an accidental decision; Amber had great cultural and historical significance in the area. It had been used for centuries in Russia for a variety of uses, including jewelry, religious relics, and ornamental things.

The Amber Room's usage of amber was a tribute to Russia's rich cultural legacy, a respect to the centuries-old tradition of amber crafting. The inclusion of this gemstone was not just an aesthetic choice but also a purposeful attempt to tie the space with Russia's historical identity.

The Masterful Artistry of Schlüter and Rastrelli

Andreas Schlüter and Bartolomeo Rastrelli were the architects tasked with designing the Amber Room. These two people each contributed their own set of abilities and views to the project, resulting in a harmonic synthesis of styles and ideas.

Andreas Schlüter, a sculptor and architect from Germany, has a background in both art and architecture. He was well-known for his inventive designs and knowledge of Baroque and Rococo aesthetic ideas. Schlüter's contribution to the Amber space was his ability to envisage the entire design of the space, elegantly merging architectural aspects with ornamental accents.

Italian architect Bartolomeo Rastrelli had already earned a name for himself in Russia with his Baroque architectural masterpieces. His work was marked by extravagant elaboration and grandeur, and his effect on Russian Baroque architecture was substantial. Rastrelli's involvement in the Amber Room project was to instill it with the luxury and splendor associated with Russian Baroque.

Schlüter and Rastrelli collaborated to develop a concept for the Amber Room that was nothing short of stunning. Their partnership would produce a space that flawlessly combines architectural innovation with aesthetic splendor.

The Craftsmen and Their Amber Alchemy

While the architects designed the Amber Room, it was the talented artisans who lovingly brought it to life. The Amber Room's heart was in its amber panels, which had to be made with the finest accuracy and elegance.

Gottfried Wolfram and Ernst Schacht, two German craftsmen, were tasked with creating the amber panels. These artisans were experts in their industry, having spent years working with amber, a substance recognized for its fragility and delicacy. The panels were made from six tons of amber, which needed not just technical competence but also a knowledge of the material's unique properties.

With its warm and transparent appearance, amber posed both obstacles and possibilities. To achieve a beautiful combination of colors and textures, the artisans had to pick and shape each piece of amber meticulously. They had to work with the amber's inherent faults and inclusions to create elaborate reliefs and mosaics that would catch the eye.

The space was not just ornamented with amber. The panels were then embellished with gilding, mirrors, and diamonds. These adornments added layers of grandeur and intricacy to the decor of the space. The area came alive with a dazzling glow as light played across the amber and gold leaf, creating an otherworldly environment that left guests in wonder.

Wolfram and Schacht's approaches were innovative for their time. Because of the fragile nature of amber, they had to devise novel ways to shape and handle it without causing harm. To obtain the appropriate amount of detail and depth in the amber panels, they experimented with several methods ranging from carving to inlay work.

As the panels formed, it became clear that the Amber Room would be more than simply a beautiful room. It was on its way to becoming a masterpiece that pushed the frontiers of art and artistry.

The Room That Defied Imagination

The Amber Room's completion was more than just the fulfillment of a creative vision; it was the realization of a dream that had stretched the limits of aesthetic and technological ability. With its amber panels, gilt accents, and exquisite mirrors, the chamber defied conception.

The Amber Room's final design was a symphony of hues and textures. Amber's warm tones harmonized effortlessly with the gold gilding, producing a rich and welcoming ambiance. Mirrors strategically placed on the walls added a feeling of space and light to the area, making it look bigger and more captivating than its actual proportions.

Every single inch of the Amber Room reflected the commitment and craftsmanship of those who had worked on it. The amber panels' exquisite reliefs and mosaics represented subjects from mythology, nature, and Russian folklore. These elements layered meaning and symbolism into the space, encouraging spectators to discover its tales and mysteries.

The Amber Room was not built overnight; it was a work of love that took many years. Every part of the space reflected the rigorous attention to detail, quest for excellence, and unshakable devotion to artistry. It was a tribute to the era's spirit of creative inventiveness.

As the Amber Room inside the Sunstone Palace

approached completion, expectation and enthusiasm surged. It was meant to become a symbol of Russian creativity, a display of the country's cultural resources, and a tribute to the imperial court's extravagance. Nobody could have predicted that this space, born of ambition and ingenuity, would captivate the hearts and minds of people all over the globe for centuries to come.

In the next chapter, I will continue our tour through the Amber Room, diving further into the artistry that distinguished its development. I will reveal the secrets of the amber, gold, and gemstone selections, as well as the confluence of styles and influences that brought this incredible space to life. The Amber Room's narrative is one of ingenuity, ambition, and unrivaled creativity, and I've just started to uncover its secrets.

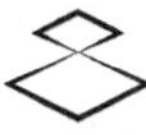

CHAPTER 2

Golden Enigma: The Craftsmanship Behind the Amber Room

In the last chapter, I investigated the Amber Room's beginnings inside the magnificent Sunstone Palace, as well as the cultural and architectural environment that set the scene for its development. Now, I will go further into the heart of this extraordinary work of art, examining the meticulous artistry and aesthetic genius that distinguished the Amber Room. I will also reveal the secrets of the amber, gold, and gemstone selections, as well as the combination of styles and influences that brought this incredible space to life.

The Essence of Craftsmanship

The Amber Room is a tribute to the achievements of

human artistry. At its heart, this chamber is a tribute to the talent, patience, and craftsmanship of the artisans who worked on it. It's a symphony of precise detail, a visual feast of amber, gold, and jewels that will take your breath away.

<u>The Mastery of Amber</u>

Amber, the Amber Room's core feature, was crucial to its entire design and appearance. The usage of amber set the area distinct, making it unique among Europe's stately halls and rooms.

Amber is a warm, golden-colored fossilized resin. It is valued for its transparency, which enables it to collect and reflect light in ways that few other materials can. Amber takes on an ethereal light when expertly cut and polished, emitting a warmth and brilliance that is really captivating.

The artisans who shaped the Amber Room's amber panels were not dealing with ordinary material. Amber is both brittle and delicate, requiring extreme care and talent to create exquisite reliefs and mosaics. To create the required appearance, every cut, carve, and polish has to be accomplished precisely.

The Allure of Gold

A heavy use of gold leaf complemented the amber in the Amber Room. Gold, which has long been associated with riches and luxury, was chosen to highlight the richness of the room's design. The gilding provided a touch of extravagance to the space, elevating it to a degree of grandeur worthy of Russian nobility.

The gold leaf was painstakingly placed on the room's surfaces, producing a glittering look that danced in the candlelight. It accentuated the warm tones of the amber, resulting in a pleasing contrast between the two materials. The combination of gold and amber was a vital component of the room's aesthetic attractiveness, and it demanded nothing short of remarkable artistry.

Gemstone Accents

Gemstones were skillfully included in the construction of the Amber Room to enhance its splendor further. These valuable stones, chosen for their hue and brightness, brought a splash of color and glitter to the amber and gold.

Agate, topaz, and quartz gemstones were utilized to create elaborate designs and ornaments on the amber panels. These gemstone embellishments offered a level of intricacy to the design, enticing visitors to explore the rich tapestry of hues and textures that decorated the room's surfaces.

The Artistic Brilliance

The Amber Room was a piece of art in its most accurate form, not just a demonstration of artistry. Every square inch of the area was a blank canvas for creative expression, and the artisans took full advantage of the chance to create a masterpiece that defied convention.

The Narrative of Relief

The Amber Room's amber panels were embellished with elaborate reliefs that portrayed a fascinating story. These reliefs showed a diverse variety of topics, from mythological and natural settings to historical and symbolic elements. Each relief was a little masterpiece in and of itself, demanding meticulous attention to detail.

The reliefs were not only for decoration; they were intended to engage the observer, urging them to investigate the tales and symbols contained inside the amber. Every feature of the reliefs, from the tiny tendrils of vegetation to the realistic representation of humans, was a monument to the artisans's talent and vision.

The Fusion of Styles

The Amber Room was not created in a single aesthetic style; instead, it welcomed a combination of styles and influences. This eclectic design approach reflected the century in which it was constructed, an era that embraced the merging of creative traditions from throughout Europe.

The Amber Room's design was inspired by the Rococo style, which emphasized rich embellishment and asymmetry. However, aspects of the Baroque and Neoclassical styles were also included in this framework, resulting in a visually vibrant and harmonious composition.

The combination of styles enabled the artisans to experiment with a wide variety of creative methods and themes. It resulted in a space that was both coherent and complex, a monument to the artists' creative freedom and creativity.

The Secrets of Selection

The Amber Room's materials were chosen with both beauty and meaning in mind. The decisions taken in this respect gave layers of meaning and value to the space, transforming it from a beautiful chamber to a cultural and aesthetic treasure.

The Significance of Amber

Long before it was integrated into the Amber Room, amber had a unique position in Russian culture. It was seen as a sign of longevity, safety, and warmth. Amber was also connected with the sun, making it an appropriate option for a space that would be lit by candlelight, providing a warm and welcoming atmosphere.

The use of amber in the Amber Room was not an accident; it was a purposeful reference to Russia's cultural history. It linked the chamber to regional customs and symbols, cementing its identity as a particularly Russian masterpiece.

The Gilded Splendor

Gold was selected for its eternal attraction as well as its grandeur and significance. For centuries, gold has been linked with riches, power, and majesty. It was a material that exuded luxury and elegance, making it an obvious choice for a space meant to highlight the majesty of Russia's royal court.

The gilding on the room's surfaces created a visual richness that complimented the amber's warmth. The combination of gold and amber was a marriage of materials that reflected both richness and tradition, resulting in a visually fascinating contrast.

Gemstones as Accents

The gemstones used in the Amber Room were not picked at random; instead, each stone was chosen for its distinct properties and meaning. Agate, for example, was utilized to create elaborate patterns that provided depth and texture to the amber panels because of its different hues and banding.

Quartz, which is recognized for its purity and brightness, was utilized to create glittering accents that reflected light and provided a sense of magic to the space. The gemstone embellishments were positioned with care to lure the eye and create focus points within the overall design.

The Enigma of Craftsmanship

I have delved into a mystery as I investigate the artistry behind the Amber Room — a blend of creativity, symbolism, and ingenuity that defies simple explanations. The room is more than simply a physical place; it represents human creativity and desire.

In the next chapter, I will explore further the Amber Room's historical journey, tracing it back to the Catherine Palace in Tsarskoye Selo. I will discuss the room's function as a symbol of Russian riches and political power, as well as its cultural and sociological effect throughout the Russian Empire. The Amber Room's narrative spans ages and countries, and its secrets and charms continue to enchant us.

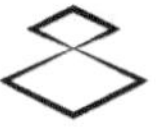

CHAPTER 3

The Tsar's Treasure: The Amber Room in the Russian Empire

In earlier chapters, I explored the Amber Room's roots inside the Sunstone Palace, the artistry that characterized its development, and the meticulous selection of materials that brought it to life. Our voyage takes us further into history as I follow the Amber Room's incredible journey to Tsarskoye Selo's Catherine Palace, where it would become a symbol of Russian grandeur and political power. I will also look at the cultural and sociological significance of this fantastic space under the Russian Empire.

From Sunstone Palace to Catherine Palace, a Royal Journey

The Amber Room's move from the Sunstone Palace

to the Catherine Palace represented a watershed point in its history. It was a voyage that would define the fate of the chamber and raise it to the rank of national treasure.

The Move to Tsarskoye Selo

In 1755, about two decades after the Amber Room was completed, Empress Elizabeth of Russia decided to relocate the masterpiece from the Sunstone Palace to the Catherine Palace at Tsarskoye Selo, just outside St. Petersburg. This was not a hasty choice; it represented the empress' wish to exhibit the chamber in a setting worthy of its majesty.

The Catherine Palace, named for Empress Elizabeth's mother, Catherine I, was a work of Russian Baroque architecture in and of itself. It had a blue and white tiled façade, sumptuous interiors, and beautiful grounds. The palace provided a superb setting for the majesty of the Amber Room, and its luxury equaled that of European courts.

The Amber Room's transfer was a complicated and sensitive procedure. The delicate amber panels had to be carefully removed, relocated, and rebuilt in their new home. The work needed the knowledge of professional artisans who had been engaged in the original design of the space.

<u>A Room Reborn</u>

The Amber Room was revived upon its arrival in the Catherine Palace. Its amber panels, precisely assembled once again, now graced a more extensive and more magnificent room. The proportions of the chamber had been increased to fit its new location better, enabling guests to have a more immersive and awe-inspiring experience.

The Amber Room was set against an opulent setting given by the Catherine Palace. The furnishings, which included gilded moldings, crystal chandeliers, and frescoed ceilings, added to the room's luxury. The warm amber tones and elaborate gold leaf embellishments in the chamber now blended seamlessly with the grandeur of the castle, creating a visual symphony of wealth and beauty.

The Amber space's relocation was more than just a change of scenery; it was a makeover that lifted the space to new heights of splendor. It was now a significant diamond in the Catherine Palace's crown, and its presence enhanced the appeal of the whole estate.

The Symbol of Russian Opulence and Power

The Amber Room, presently housed inside the Catherine Palace, became a symbol of Russian grandeur and political power. Its presence in the palace was a statement of the Russian Empire's strength and riches, as well as a monument to the splendor of the royal court.

The Splendors of Imperial Russia

Russia had an era of cultural and political triumph under the reigns of Empress Elizabeth and, subsequently, Catherine the Great. The empire was growing, and the Russian court was becoming more international. The Amber Room played a critical part in Russia's monarchs' aim to emulate the courts of Europe.

With its expensive materials and elaborate design, the Amber Room showed Russia's aesthetic and creative capabilities. It displayed the empire's capacity to equal the grandeur of European courts and reflected Russia's expanding global dominance.

A Amber Room

Political Significance

The Amber Room has political importance in addition to its position as a showcase of luxury. It was often utilized to hold major diplomatic gatherings and celebrations. Foreign dignitaries who visited the Catherine Palace were treated to this beautiful hall, which left them with no question about Russia's might and grandeur.

The luxury of the chamber reflected the empire's capacity to command enormous resources and exercise influence on the world stage. It was more than just a piece of art; it was a diplomatic instrument and a symbol of Russia's status among the world's major nations.

Cultural and Societal Impact

The Amber Room's existence in the Catherine Palace had a tremendous cultural and sociological influence on Russia. Both the Russian elite and the average public were fascinated, inspired, and even obsessed with it.

A Cultural Marvel

The Amber space was more than simply a space; it was a cultural masterpiece that captivated everyone who saw it. Visitors from all around Europe and beyond were amazed by its beauty and precise artistry. It quickly became a must-see destination for both visitors and dignitaries.

The complex reliefs, gemstone accents, and gold gilding of the chamber spawned a wave of creative and decorative developments throughout Russia. The Amber Room's design might be observed in architecture, home décor, and even fashion during the period.

A National Treasure

The Amber Room became a symbol of national pride as it rose in popularity within Russian culture. It was hailed as a triumph of Russian aesthetic accomplishment and innovation. The chamber did not belong to the imperial court; it belonged to the Russian people.

The Amber Room became an essential component of Russian identity, serving as a symbol of the country's cultural legacy. It was a source of pride for a nation keen to demonstrate its global standing. The importance of the space extended beyond its physical existence; it was a symbol of Russia's rich history and creative tradition.

A Source of Intrigue and Mystery

While the Amber Room was in the limelight, it was also cloaked in mystery and intrigue. The mystery surrounding the room's origins, the secrets of its quality, and its deep symbolism captivated both researchers and the general public.

As the chamber grew in popularity, it drew its fair share of conjecture and intrigue. The Amber Room's intriguing attraction was enhanced by stories of buried wealth, forgotten secrets, and even curses. The room's complicated history and the mysteries surrounding it further added to its cultural significance.

The Amber Room's Enduring Legacy

Chapter 3 took us from the Sunstone Palace to the Catherine Palace, chronicling the evolution of the Amber Room became a symbol of Russian grandeur and political power. I've looked at how it influenced culture and society under the Russian Empire, from influencing creative movements to being a source of national pride and mystery.

With its rich history and long influence, the Amber

Room is more than simply an architectural marvel; it is a tribute to the complicated interaction of art, politics, and culture. I will dive into the circumstances behind its unexplained disappearance during World War II and the ensuing quest for this lost treasure as I continue the examination of its narrative. The Amber Room's voyage has been filled with intrigue and mystery, and its story is far from done.

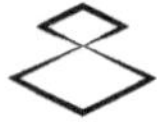

CHAPTER 4

Lost Luminescence: The Disappearance During World War II

I have followed the Amber Room from the Sunstone Palace to the Catherine Palace, where it became a symbol of Russian grandeur and political power. The story takes a dramatic turn now as I uncover the circumstances that led to the inexplicable disappearance of the Amber Room during WWII. I will look at the turmoil of conflict, the frantic attempts to safeguard cultural artifacts, and the aftermath and early quest for the lost masterpiece.

Prelude to Darkness

The start of World War II in 1939 threw a lengthy shadow over Europe and, later, the Amber Room. The destiny of the chamber was in doubt as Nazi armies pushed into Eastern Europe. The delicate artistry and precious materials of the chamber made it a prominent target for looting, and its destruction became a top goal for Soviet officials.

Preservation Efforts

Recognizing the impending danger, Soviet curators and conservators launched measures to protect the Amber Room. The amber panels in the room were meticulously covered with wallpaper, and the gold leaf was masked with paint to prevent looting or damage. Other significant artworks and cultural objects from the Catherine Palace were also evacuated, and a comprehensive strategy to conserve Russia's artistic legacy was put in place.

However, as the conflict progressed, the capacity to safeguard these valuables became more difficult. The oncoming Nazi armies presented a danger not just to the Amber Room but to European cultural heritage as a whole.

The Nazi Occupation

Nazi Germany launched Operation Barbarossa, an invasion of the Soviet Union, in 1941. The Nazis reached Tsarskoye Selo and the Catherine Palace as they stormed across Eastern Europe. As the Nazis took the castle and claimed its valuables, the destiny of the Amber Room hung in the balance.

The Looting of Tsarskoye Selo

The Nazi administration, led by Reichsmarschall Hermann Göring, was methodical and brutal in its plundering of artworks and cultural artifacts across Europe. The Amber Room was no exception to this plundering expedition.

German troops uncovered the hidden panels in the chamber, and their actual worth was instantly understood. The Amber Room's amber, gold, and gemstone features made it an impossible treasure to pass up. The panels were removed, crated, and sent to Königsberg (now Kaliningrad, Russia), where they would be lost to history.

The Enigma of Königsberg

The fate of the Amber Room after its relocation to Königsberg remains one of World War II's biggest mysteries. As the war came to an end, the location of the chamber became the focus of considerable curiosity and study.

Despite intensive searches and inquiries, the location of the chamber remained a mystery. Over the years, other ideas and allegations have developed, with some claiming that it was buried in underground bunkers or relocated to secret sites. The Amber Room had gone into thin air, leaving a vacuum in the realm of art and cultural heritage.

The Aftermath and the Quest for Answers

With the conclusion of World War II came a strong desire to reclaim and restore the artifacts looted during the fight. The Soviet authorities were desperate to find and restore this lost masterpiece to its proper location, and the Amber Room was at the forefront of their efforts.

The Nuremberg Trials

The Nuremberg Trials were conducted in the wake of World War II to bring Nazi war criminals to justice. These trials also revealed the magnitude of Nazi plunder and the fate of stolen artworks such as the Amber Room.

Several high-ranking Nazi officers were questioned regarding the Amber Room's location, but none were able or willing to offer clear answers. As various tales and assertions arose, the mystery surrounding the room's removal grew.

The Cold War and Diplomatic Efforts

The Cold War that followed World War II made the quest for the Amber Room more difficult. The split postwar world made East-West collaboration difficult, and the room's recovery remained elusive.

Diplomatic attempts, however, persisted, and conversations concerning the likely location of the chamber were undertaken between Soviet and Western authorities. According to multiple leads and intelligence sources, the chamber may be concealed in a variety of places, including underground bunkers, caverns, or even submerged in the Baltic Sea.

The Search Continues

The quest for the Amber Room lasted decades, with periodic excursions and studies seeking to locate it. The chamber remained secret despite the painstaking efforts of specialists, historians, and treasure seekers.

The Amber Room became the stuff of legend and folklore as the years passed. It captivated the minds of artists, authors, and historians, sparking fresh interest in the mystery surrounding its disappearance.

The Cultural and Emotional Impact

The loss of the Amber Room during WWII had far-reaching cultural and emotional ramifications. The demise of the chamber left an enduring impression on the worlds of art and cultural heritage.

Cultural Loss

The Amber Room was more than an architectural marvel; it represented creative excellence and a cultural legacy. Its disappearance was seen as a tragedy not just for Russia but for the whole globe. The space had captivated individuals from all walks of life, and its disappearance created a hole in the worlds of art and history.

The disappearance of the chamber had a significant cultural influence on Russia. It was a stark reminder of war's devastation and the ruin of valuable cultural assets. Attempts to reclaim the space became a symbol of tenacity and commitment to redress a historical injustice.

Emotional Toll

The emotional impact of the Amber Room's

disappearance went well beyond art and culture. It was a narrative that touched millions of people's hearts and piqued their interest.

Families who had lived through the war recalled visiting the Catherine Palace and marveling at the magnificence of the chamber. The chamber had been a source of pride and astonishment for the family, and its demise was a bitter reminder of a bygone age.

The mystery of the room's destiny tormented art historians and fans. The hunt for answers became motivated by a strong emotional attachment to the space and a desire to learn the truth.

The Vanishing Enigma

The fourth part delves into the Amber Room's worst chapter — its disappearance during World War II. I have researched the Nazi pillage of the Catherine Palace, the mystery of the room's fate in Königsberg, and the following hunt for explanations.

The Amber Room had disappeared into the depths of history, once a beacon of grandeur and creative brilliance.

Decades of laborious investigation, worldwide collaboration, and a never-ending hunt for answers would be required to solve the riddle of its disappearance.

In the following chapters, I will investigate the many ideas and stories surrounding the Amber Room's destiny, ranging from conspiracy theories to espionage, as well as the emotional toll and worldwide fascination with this unresolved enigma. The narrative of The Amber Room is one of mystery and intrigue, and it continues to fascinate the world's imagination.

CHAPTER 5

The Amber Enigma: Theories and Legends Surrounding the Lost Room

In the previous chapters, I delved into the disappearance of the Amber Room during World War II and the subsequent search for this lost masterpiece. Now, our journey takes us into the realm of intrigue and speculation as we explore the myriad theories and legends concerning the Amber Room's fate. We will uncover conspiracy theories, espionage, and the shadowy world of art theft, shedding light on the emotional toll and global fascination with this mystery.

The Amber Room's Vanishing Act

The Amber Room's disappearance remains one of the greatest mysteries in the world of art and cultural heritage.

Its vanishing act has given rise to numerous theories and speculations, each offering a different perspective on its fate.

The Theories

- **Nazi Looting:** The most widely accepted theory is that Nazi forces looted the Amber Room during their occupation of the Catherine Palace in Tsarskoye Selo. According to this theory, the panels were transported to Königsberg, where they were lost during the city's bombardment.

- **Hidden in Bunkers:** Some theories suggest that the room was hidden in underground bunkers or tunnels to protect it from the advancing Soviet forces. These theories often point to the vast network of tunnels and bunkers constructed by the Nazis during the war.

- **Sunk in the Baltic Sea:** Another theory proposes that the Amber Room was transported to a ship and deliberately sunk in the Baltic Sea to prevent its discovery. This theory draws on reports of wartime submarine activity and the Baltic's murky depths.

- **Smuggled to Safety:** Accounts are suggesting that the panels of the Amber Room were smuggled out of Königsberg before its fall. This theory speculates that the room was divided and transported to various locations for safekeeping.

- **Lost in Fires:** Some believe that the Amber Room was destroyed in the fires that engulfed Königsberg during the final days of the war. The chaos and destruction of the city made it challenging to preserve valuable items.

Espionage and Intrigue

The disappearance of the Amber Room has also given rise to espionage and intrigue, adding layers of complexity to the mystery.

- **The Spy Connection:** Espionage plays a role in several theories surrounding the Amber Room's fate. Some believe that spies, both Soviet and Western, were involved in the room's removal or concealment. The Cold War era was marked by espionage and covert operations, and some viewed the Amber Room's disappearance as a high-stakes geopolitical maneuver.

- **Secret Documents:** Declassified documents from various intelligence agencies have fueled speculation about the Amber Room's fate. These documents, often heavily redacted, have been the subject of intense scrutiny by researchers and historians seeking clues about the room's whereabouts.

- **Double Agents and Deception:** Some theories propose that double agents may have played a role in the Amber Room's disappearance. These theories suggest that individuals with allegiances to multiple sides of the conflict may have been involved in secret operations related to the room.

The Emotional Toll

The Amber Room's enigmatic disappearance has taken an emotional toll on those who have dedicated their lives to unraveling its mystery. The quest to find the room has been marked by frustration, disappointment, and a deep emotional connection to the lost treasure.

- **Frustration and Dead Ends:** Decades of searches, expeditions, and investigations have yielded little concrete evidence about the room's fate. Many researchers and historians have encountered frustration as they follow leads that ultimately lead to dead ends.

- **Personal Connections:** The Amber Room's story has touched the lives of countless individuals who feel a personal connection to its mystery. Families who remember visiting the Catherine Palace before the war or hearing stories from relatives who lived through that era have a deep emotional stake in uncovering the truth.

- **Dedicated Researchers:** Historians, art restorers, and treasure hunters have dedicated their careers to solving the Amber Room's mystery. Their tireless efforts reflect a commitment to preserving cultural heritage and uncovering the truth about this lost masterpiece.

Global Fascination

The Amber Room's disappearance has captivated the world's imagination, transcending national boundaries and becoming a symbol of both cultural loss and the enduring quest for answers.

Literary and Artistic Inspiration

The Amber Room's mystery has inspired numerous works of literature, art, and film. Writers have woven tales of intrigue and adventure around the room's disappearance, adding layers of fiction to the real-life mystery. Artists have captured the room's beauty in paintings, and filmmakers have brought its story to the silver screen. These creative expressions have kept the Amber Room's memory alive in the public consciousness.

Conspiracy Theories

Conspiracy theories about the Amber Room have increased over the years, adding to the room's allure and mystique. Some theories suggest that a secret society hid the room, while others propose that it holds the key to hidden treasures or ancient mysteries. These theories, though often lacking in verifiable evidence, continue to fuel fascination with the room.

International Collaborations

The search for the Amber Room has fostered international collaborations and partnerships. Experts and organizations from around the world have joined efforts to locate and recover the room. This global cooperation reflects the room's status as a shared cultural treasure and the collective desire to solve its mystery.

Tourist Attraction

The Amber Room's story has turned the Catherine Palace into a significant tourist attraction. Visitors from around the world flock to the palace not only to admire its opulence but also to ponder the mysteries of the vanished masterpiece. The room's absence has become as much a part of its story as its presence once was.

The Unending Quest

Chapter 5 explores the vast landscape of theories and legends surrounding the Amber Room's fate. From Nazi looting to espionage and conspiracy theories, the room's disappearance remains an enigma that continues to captivate the world's imagination.

As we move forward in our exploration of the Amber Room's story, I will delve into the monumental task of reconstructing the room after its vanishing act, shedding light on the international collaboration, thorough research, and dedication involved. The Amber Room's journey is one of resilience and historical preservation, and its tale is far from over. 45

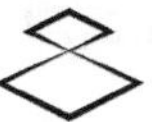

CHAPTER 6

Rekindling the Flame: The Reconstruction and Legacy of the Amber Room

We traveled through the Amber Room's remarkable history in earlier chapters, from its beginnings in the Sunstone Palace to its inexplicable disappearance during World War II. I will now shift our focus to a narrative of rebirth and perseverance, chronicling the mammoth undertaking of rebuilding the Amber Room following its disappearance. We will examine the room's second life as a symbol of resilience and historical preservation, as well as the worldwide teamwork, meticulous study, and commitment that went into it.

The Impossible Task

Following the conclusion of World War II, the

recovery of stolen art masterpieces, notably the Amber Room, became a key priority. The massive undertaking of reconstruction started with a modest but bold goal: to bring back to life a vanished art masterpiece.

The Hunt for Clues

The initial stage in the rebuilding endeavor was to collect as much information on the original Amber Room as possible. Decades of investigation went into searching through archives, records, and images. Historians, art experts, and academics combed the world for any clues that may help in the resuscitation of the chamber.

International Collaboration

Rebuilding the Amber Room was a genuinely global project. Experts and fans from Russia, Germany, and other countries gathered in the spirit of collaboration and shared cultural legacy. This collective effort attested to the Amber Room's ongoing attractiveness and value as a symbol of creative excellence.

The Puzzling Task

It was like putting together a massive jigsaw with innumerable missing parts to recreate the Amber Room.

The complex design, meticulous artistry, and unusual materials of the space posed a unique challenge.

Amber Is Missing

The disappearance of the original amber panels was one of the most severe issues. The valuable amber that had graced the chamber had been lost to history, leaving artisans with the difficult job of reproducing it. Amber specialists were contacted, and great care was taken to locate and utilize amber of the same grade and hue as the original.

Painstaking Craftsmanship

The Amber Room's renovation needed a fantastic degree of artistry and attention. Each panel was painstakingly carved, painted, and gilded by artisans to match the original design. The delicate features, from the floral designs to the gilt moldings, had to be meticulously replicated.

A Labor of Love

The Amber Room's restoration was more than just an aesthetic undertaking; it was a labor of love and a testimony to human perseverance.

Artisans and Craftsmen

Skilled artisans and craftsmen worked for years to recreate the Amber Room. These people admired the original work and were motivated by a desire to commemorate its legacy. Each brushstroke, each golden detail, expressed their dedication to preserving history.

Historical Accuracy

In the reconstruction effort, historical accuracy was critical. To guarantee that every feature of the space was authentically reconstructed, researchers reviewed historical records, pictures, and eyewitness reports. The objective was to represent not just the aesthetic of the Amber Room but also its soul and character.

The Unveiling

The rebuilt Amber Room was shown to the public after years of diligent effort. The historic event culminated decades of study, cooperation, and artistry.

Return to Tsarskoye Selo

The Amber Room acquired a new home at Tsarskoye Selo's Catherine Palace, where it had gone during World War II. Its reappearance was a strong signal of survival and historical preservation.

A Global Sensation

The restored Amber Room rapidly became a worldwide phenomenon. Visitors from all over the globe came to see the stunning reconstruction of this lost masterpiece at the Catherine Palace. It was more than just a space; it was a symbol of victory over hardship and a monument to art's and culture's eternal power.

The Legacy of the Amber Room

The Amber Room's significance goes beyond its physical rebuilding. Its imprint on the worlds of art, history, and cultural heritage is indelible.

A Symbol of Resilience

The Amber Room's journey from oblivion to resurrection has made it a symbol of tenacity. It is a monument to people and countries' persistent commitment to preserve their cultural riches in the face of immense tragedy.

Cultural Diplomacy

The restored Amber Room has helped to develop goodwill and cooperation between Russia and other countries via cultural diplomacy. It acts as a bridge of understanding, reminding people throughout the globe of the need to conserve and safeguard our shared cultural legacy.

A Source of Inspiration

The Amber Room is still inspiring painters, authors, and historians. Its narrative of tragedy and recovery, mystery and tenacity, has captivated generations. It is a reminder of art's eternal potential to transcend time and suffering.

The Eternal Flame

Chapter 6 chronicles the monumental task of reconstructing the Amber Room after its vanishing act. The endeavor to reconstruct this forgotten masterpiece was a labor of love and a triumph of the human spirit, from the arduous study to the committed artistry.

As I continue the investigation of the Amber Room's history, I will consider its modern importance, as well as

A Amber Room

its effect on popular culture, art, and historical memory. The Amber Room's legacy is one of eternal curiosity, and its narrative lives on in the annals of time.

CHAPTER 7

Contemporary Significance: The Amber Room in the Modern World

As we delve deeper into the story of the Amber Room, we come to a chapter that explores its contemporary significance. Beyond its historical roots, the Amber Room has a profound impact on the modern world. In this chapter, we will reflect on the ongoing cultural significance of the Amber Room, examine its influence on popular culture, art, and historical memory, and discuss its role in contemporary Russia and its place on the global stage.

A Timeless Treasure

The Amber Room's allure is timeless, and its cultural significance persists through the ages. In today's world, it continues to captivate the imagination and serves as a symbol of both artistic achievement and the enduring quest for answers.

A Living Legacy

The Amber Room is not merely an artifact of the past; it is a living legacy that bridges the gap between history and contemporary culture. Its existence today stands as a testament to the power of art and human determination.

Cultural Tourism

The Catherine Palace, home to the Amber Room, has become a significant tourist attraction. Visitors from around the world flock to Tsarskoye Selo to witness the reconstructed masterpiece, underscoring its enduring appeal and cultural significance.

Influence on Popular Culture

The Amber Room's mysterious history and radiant beauty have made it a popular subject in various forms of media, from literature to film. It has left an indelible mark on popular culture.

Literary Inspiration

Writers have been drawn to the Amber Room's

mystique. Numerous novels and historical fiction works have been penned, weaving tales of adventure and intrigue around the lost masterpiece. This literary fascination keeps the Amber Room's story alive in the minds of readers.

Cinematic Representation

The Amber Room has made its way onto the silver screen, further cementing its status in popular culture. Movies and documentaries have explored its history, disappearance, and reconstruction, allowing audiences to immerse themselves in its enigmatic tale.

Artistic Expression

Artists, too, have been inspired by the Amber Room's radiant beauty. Paintings and artworks have sought to capture its grandeur, ensuring that its image endures as a work of art in itself.

Historical Memory

The Amber Room's story is a testament to the impact of war on cultural heritage. Its disappearance during World War II serves as a reminder of the devastating consequences of conflict on art and history.

Lessons from the Past

The loss of the Amber Room during the war serves as a poignant lesson in the preservation of cultural treasures. It underscores the importance of safeguarding art and historical artifacts during times of conflict.

Commemoration and Remembrance

The Amber Room's disappearance is commemorated annually, not only in Russia but also in other parts of the world. These events serve as a reminder of the importance of preserving cultural heritage and the ongoing quest to recover lost treasures.

Contemporary Russia and the Global Stage

The Amber Room holds a unique place in contemporary Russia and the global cultural landscape. It serves as a symbol of national pride and has a role to play on the international stage.

A Symbol of Russian Heritage

In Russia, the Amber Room is a symbol of national heritage and resilience. Its reconstruction represents the nation's commitment to preserving its rich cultural history, even in the face of adversity.

Cultural Diplomacy

The Amber Room has played a role in cultural diplomacy, fostering international cooperation and goodwill. Exhibitions and collaborations related to the Amber Room have strengthened Russia's cultural ties with other nations.

Global Fascination

The Amber Room's story continues to captivate people from all corners of the world. Its allure transcends borders and serves as a testament to the universal appeal of art and history.

A Timeless Legacy

Chapter 7 has explored the contemporary significance of the Amber Room, from its enduring cultural allure to its influence on popular culture, art, and historical memory. It has also highlighted its role in contemporary Russia and on the global stage.

As I prepare to conclude our journey through the Amber Room's history and significance, we will reflect on the captivating journey of this cultural treasure, from its creation to its disappearance and resurrection. The Amber

A Amber Room

Room's legacy is one of enduring fascination, reminding us that art and history are timeless treasures that continue to enrich our lives and connect us to the past.

The Amber Room stands as a testament to the human spirit's resilience and determination to preserve and celebrate the beauty of the past in the present. It is a symbol of the power of art and culture to transcend time and adversity, leaving an indelible mark on those who have the privilege to experience its magnificence.

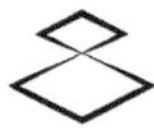

CHAPTER 8

Conclusion

In this last part, we will review the enthralling narrative of the Amber Room, from its birth in the Sunstone Palace to its strange absence during WWII and victorious reappearance. We will conclude by reflecting on the room's persistent fascination and posing concerns regarding the room's eventual fate and the continuous hunt for solutions.

The Amber Room's Journey

The journey of The Amber Room is nothing short of miraculous. It's a narrative of creative genius, cultural importance, grief, perseverance, and the never-ending search for truth.

Creation in the Sunstone Palace

The Sunstone Palace's magnificent setting gave birth

to the Amber Room. Artisans of unrivaled talent and vision created this masterwork of amber, gold, and jewels. It was a tribute to the Russian Empire's grandeur and devotion to creative quality.

The Russian Empire

The Amber Room became more than simply a magnificent piece of art during its period in the Russian Empire; it signified the riches and authority of the Russian tsars. It was a venue where the policy was formed, and dignitaries were impressed. It was an essential aspect of Russian culture.

Disappearance During World War II

World War II cast a terrible shadow on the Amber Room's history. Its unexpected disappearance remains one of the art world's biggest mysteries. Despite the war's turmoil and destruction, the memory of the chamber survived, and the mission to discover it never wavered.

The Mysteries and Legends

The Amber Room became enveloped in mystery and folklore throughout the years. Theories concerning its demise ranged from Nazi plunder to espionage and hidden lairs. These stories further contributed to the room's attraction, making it a worldwide mystery.

The Reconstruction

The Amber Room repair was a massive undertaking that took years and included worldwide cooperation. Skilled artisans and craftsmen worked painstakingly to reproduce the delicate beauty of the space. The world saw a victory of art, culture, and human willpower when it was revealed.

The Enduring Allure

The attraction of the Amber Room is eternal. It has stood the test of time, wars, and political administrations. But what is it about this cultural gem that keeps it so fascinating?

Beauty Beyond Measure

The Amber Room is breathtaking in every way. Its beautifully carved amber panels, gilt moldings, and jewel-like detailing are proof of human creative prowess. It is a piece of art that speaks to people from all walks of life and civilizations.

The Power of Mystery

Mystery has a unique ability to capture the human imagination. The mystery behind the disappearance of the Amber Room, as well as the different ideas and stories that have evolved, keep its narrative alive and its appeal ever-present.

Resilience and Triumph

The Amber Room's narrative is one of perseverance and victory over adversity. Its rebirth after being lost for decades serves as a source of inspiration and optimism, reminding us that art and culture can persevere even in the face of immense adversity.

Questions Unanswered

As we come to the end of our exploration of the Amber Room's history and importance, we are left with unanswered questions regarding its final fate and the continued search for answers.

What Lies Ahead?

What does the Amber Room's future hold? Will new information emerge to shed light on its enigmatic disappearance during WWII? Will it inspire artists, authors, and historians for future generations?

The Quest for Answers

The search for information about the Amber Room's destiny is continuing. Researchers, historians, and art lovers are still working hard to uncover the room's mysteries. The hunt for missing jigsaw pieces and documentation continues, spurred by the urge to finish the puzzle.

A Symbol of Human Ingenuity

The Amber Room represents human inventiveness, innovation, and perseverance. It symbolizes our capacity to produce beauty in the face of adversity, as well as our desire to maintain and defend our cultural legacy.

Final Reflection

The Amber Room's journey demonstrates the everlasting power of art and culture. It serves as a reminder that once produced, beauty can never wholly be lost. The attraction of the chamber will fascinate future generations, and its tale will remain a source of intrigue, inspiration, and hope.

A Amber Room

We are reminded of the powerful effect of art on our lives as we reflect on the enthralling story of the Amber Room, from its construction to its disappearance and resurrection. It is a treasure that transcends time and space, linking us to the past, motivating us in the present, and influencing our future.

The Amber Room's final fate is unknown, but its position in history is guaranteed. It is a cultural treasure that will continue to shine as a light of craftsmanship, perseverance, and the ever-evolving fabric of human history.

CHAPTER 9

Epilogue

In this final chapter of our journey through the captivating history of the Amber Room, we provide updates on any recent developments or discoveries related to this enigmatic cultural treasure. We also offer a closing reflection on the evolving narrative of the Amber Room's history, a story that continues to unfold and intrigue.

Recent Developments and Discoveries

The story of the Amber Room is not a closed chapter; it is an ongoing narrative that occasionally reveals new twists and turns. In recent years, several developments and discoveries have shed light on this enduring mystery.

The Amber Room's 300th Anniversary

One significant recent development was the

celebration of the Amber Room's 300th anniversary in 2023. This milestone was marked by exhibitions, events, and publications dedicated to the room's history and significance. It served as a reminder of the enduring cultural importance of this masterpiece.

Ongoing Research and Investigation

Researchers and historians have continued to delve into the Amber Room's past. Advances in technology have enabled more in-depth analysis of historical documents, photographs, and artifacts related to the room. These efforts have led to a deeper understanding of its creation and disappearance.

The Amber Room's Digital Presence

In the age of digital information, the Amber Room has also found a new platform for exploration. Online databases, virtual tours, and digital reconstructions allow enthusiasts from around the world to immerse themselves in the room's intricate beauty and history.

The Search for Missing Pieces

One of the most enduring mysteries of the Amber Room is the whereabouts of the original amber panels.

Despite decades of searching, these precious pieces remain missing. Recent efforts to locate the missing panels have reignited hopes of completing the room's restoration.

A Reflection on the Evolving Narrative

The history of the Amber Room is a tale of creation, disappearance, and resurrection, but it is also a narrative that evolves with time. As we reflect on this narrative, several key themes emerge.

The Power of Artistic Creation

The creation of the Amber Room in the 18th century was a testament to the power of artistic vision and craftsmanship. It was a symbol of the Russian Empire's cultural and creative achievements. This aspect of the narrative continues to inspire and remind us of the enduring value of artistic expression.

The Impact of War on Cultural Heritage

The disappearance of the Amber Room during World War II is a stark reminder of the devastating impact of war on cultural heritage. It serves as a call to action for the protection and preservation of art and historical artifacts during times of conflict.

The Quest for Answers

The ongoing search for answers about the Amber Room's fate is a testament to human curiosity and determination. It is a reminder that even the most enduring mysteries can be unraveled with dedication and collaborative effort.

The Room's Contemporary Significance

The Amber Room's contemporary significance is a testament to its enduring allure. It continues to captivate people from all walks of life and serves as a symbol of cultural heritage, resilience, and the power of art to transcend time.

An Unfinished Story

In closing, the story of the Amber Room remains an unfinished narrative. While we have traveled through its history, explored its significance, and reflected on recent developments, the room's ultimate destiny remains uncertain.

The Amber Room is more than just a physical space; it is a symbol of human creativity, resilience, and the enduring quest for answers. Its allure continues to inspire, and its mysteries continue to challenge. As we conclude our journey, we are reminded that the narrative of the Amber Room is a story that will continue to evolve, enriching our understanding of history and the enduring power of art and culture.

In the years to come, discoveries may illuminate the room's past, and perhaps one day, the missing amber panels will be found, completing the puzzle. Until then, the Amber Room will remain a symbol of the indomitable spirit of those who seek to uncover its secrets and celebrate its beauty—a cultural treasure that transcends time and captivates the human imagination.

A Amber Room